APPROACHABLE LEADERSHIP

Foundations of Effective

Conflict Resolution

Dustin Beasley

TABLE OF CONTENTS

INTRODUCTION

Alright, picture this. Conflict is like a vigorous game of dodgeball. It's fast, it's intense, and if you're not paying attention, you might just get hit in the face with a rubber ball. Now, don't misunderstand me; nobody is suggesting we throw balls at each other in the office (as entertaining as that might sound). No, we're talking about the idea of conflict as a necessary, and even healthy, part of leadership.

See, the thing is, leadership isn't about having a team of nodding bobbleheads. It's about fostering a group of unique individuals, each with their ideas, perspectives, and, yes, disagreements. Conflict, then, is not just inevitable; it's desirable. It's the difference between a flat soda and one that's effervescent, bursting with life and energy.

But here's the kicker. Just like in dodgeball, how you handle that flying rubber ball of conflict makes all the difference. Effective conflict management is like catching and using that ball mid-air to your advantage. It creates a vibrant environment where people can challenge ideas, foster creativity, and foster innovation. It's that electric atmosphere where everyone feels heard, valued, and motivated to give their best.

On the other hand, failing to manage conflict, or worse, avoiding it altogether, is like letting that ball smack you square in the face. It stifles communication, hampers creativity, and creates an environment of fear and stagnation. It's like trying to make a gourmet meal with only one ingredient. It's possible, but it's unlikely to win any Michelin stars.

So, let's sum it up. Conflict can be a catalyst for growth, innovation, and unity when approached with openness, respect, and a dash of humor. It's a chance for us to understand and appreciate our differences and harness them to create something truly amazing. It's not just about dodging balls; it's about catching them, throwing them, and knowing that the game is more fun when everyone gets to play.

Section 1

UNDERSTANDING CONFLICT

What is Conflict, Really?

Conflict... It's like that pesky mosquito that just won't leave you alone on a warm summer night. It buzzes around, gets in your face, and it's downright annoying. But just as mosquitoes play a crucial role in the ecosystem (like serving as a food source for a variety of animals), conflict too has its place in our lives. When handled properly, it can lead to personal growth, deeper understanding, and ultimately, positive change.

Now, let's go on a little safari and explore some specific types of conflict you might encounter in the wild plains of human interaction.

Relationship Conflict:

You know when your best friend insists on always picking the restaurant for your monthly catch-ups and you're honestly tired of Italian food? That's relationship conflict. It occurs when there are personal disagreements or clashes due to strong personalities, communication styles, or interpersonal behaviors.

Examples:

1. **Workstyle Differences:** You prefer to plan and execute tasks well in advance, while your colleague thrives under the pressure of last-minute deadlines. This difference in workstyles leads to tension and misunderstandings about project timelines.

2. **Communication Missteps:** One team member communicates primarily through email, believing it's efficient and clear, while another finds this approach impersonal and prefers face-to-face conversations. This results in feelings of disconnect and frustration.

Ask Yourself: How often do I encounter relationship conflicts? What patterns do I notice?

Action Tip: Practice empathy and open communication. Taking the time to truly understand where the other person is coming from can prevent misunderstandings and strengthen the relationship. This approach works because it addresses the emotional aspect of the conflict, not just the issue at hand.

Resource Conflict:

Ever felt like a seagull fighting over the last piece of bread? That's resource conflict for you. It happens when there are disputes over access to resources, be they tangible (like money, space, or materials) or intangible (like information or time).

Examples:

1. **The Meeting Room Melodrama**: Two teams need the same meeting room at the same time. It's like a game of musical chairs, but with more at stake than just a seat.

2. **The Printer Predicament**: There's only one printer in the office, and it's always out of ink or paper when you need it most. It's the office version of "The Hunger Games."

Ask Yourself: Do I find myself in resource conflicts at work or at home? How could they be avoided?

Action Tip: Engage in collaborative problem-solving. Look for creative solutions where both parties can have their needs met. This works because it shifts the focus from competing for limited resources to finding a way to optimize resource use for mutual benefit.

Structural Conflict:

Structural conflict is like trying to play a board game when the rules aren't clear. It happens due to power structures, hierarchies, or differing roles and responsibilities.

Examples:

1. The Hierarchy Hoedown: You're a middle manager caught between upper management's strategies and your team's ground realities. It's like being a tennis ball in a never-ending rally.

2. The Role Roulette: Your job description says one thing, but you end up doing everything but that. You're the office Swiss Army Knife, but without the cool gadgets.

Ask Yourself: Are there structural conflicts in my organization? How do they impact my work or well-being?

Action Tip: Clarify roles and responsibilities and foster open dialogue about organizational structure. This is effective because it directly addresses the root cause of the conflict – the unclear or unfair structures within the organization.

Interest Conflict:

Ever had an argument with your sibling about which TV show to watch? That's interest conflict. It arises when individuals have different needs, desires, or interests.

Examples:

1. **Project Prioritization**: You believe that the team should focus on a long-term project that could bring significant benefits to the company, but your coworker insists on prioritizing short-term tasks for immediate results. This conflict of interests affects decision-making and resource allocation.

2. **Budget Allocation**: During budget meetings, you argue for more funds to enhance the marketing department, while another manager pushes for upgrading IT

infrastructure. Both believe their interests are crucial for the company's growth, leading to a standoff.

Ask Yourself: How often do I encounter interest conflicts? How can I better manage them?

Action Tip: Focus on understanding each other's underlying needs and finding a middle ground. By identifying the real needs behind the stated positions, you can often find solutions that satisfy everyone's interests.

Values Conflict:

You're a vegan, and your partner insists on having a steak dinner at your wedding. That's a values conflict. It emerges when people have different belief systems, cultural backgrounds, or ethical standards.

Examples:

1. **Ethical Practices**: You advocate for ethically sourced materials in your production line, emphasizing corporate responsibility, while a colleague argues for more cost-effective options that may not adhere to the same ethical standards. This creates a moral

dilemma and tension over company values.

2. **Work-Life Balance**: You value a healthy work-life balance and encourage flexible working hours, while your supervisor prioritizes productivity and traditional working hours, believing it leads to better results. This clash in values affects team morale and job satisfaction.

Ask Yourself: Have I experienced a values conflict recently? How did it make me feel?

Action Tip: Respect and acknowledge each other's values while seeking common ground. This works because it builds mutual respect and understanding, which is crucial when dealing with deeply held beliefs and values.

Let's clear up a common misunderstanding: conflict isn't the bogeyman hiding under your professional bed. It's not about drawing battle lines at the water cooler or seeing who can shout the loudest in meetings. Conflict is not synonymous with 'World War III at the office.'

Also, let's talk about the 'eye of the beholder' aspect of conflict. For some, a heated discussion is just another Tuesday; for others, it's a scene straight out of a dramatic soap opera. This difference often comes down to our personal baggage - yes, we all have it. If you've been in situations where your ideas were trampled on, you might see a simple debate as a full-on attack on your intellect or person.

And then there are the outside shenanigans. Imagine juggling instructions from several bosses - one says tomato, another says tomato, and a third says, 'Why are we even talking about tomatoes?' This circus can turn what should be a straightforward task into a conflict-laden nightmare.

So remember, conflict isn't about the clash of titans or an emotional rollercoaster. It's often just a cocktail of personal filters and external chaos. Understanding this can turn the dreaded 'C-word' into just another manageable part of your workday.

Remember, conflict isn't a nasty beast to be feared. It's just a part of life. And with the right tools and understanding, you can be the intrepid explorer who navigates it with grace, wisdom, and maybe even a little bit of excitement.

Let's roll up our sleeves and get ready to dive into our own unique conflict management styles in the following modules. Remember, every conflict is an opportunity to learn, grow, and develop better relationships with those around us. Let's make the most of it!

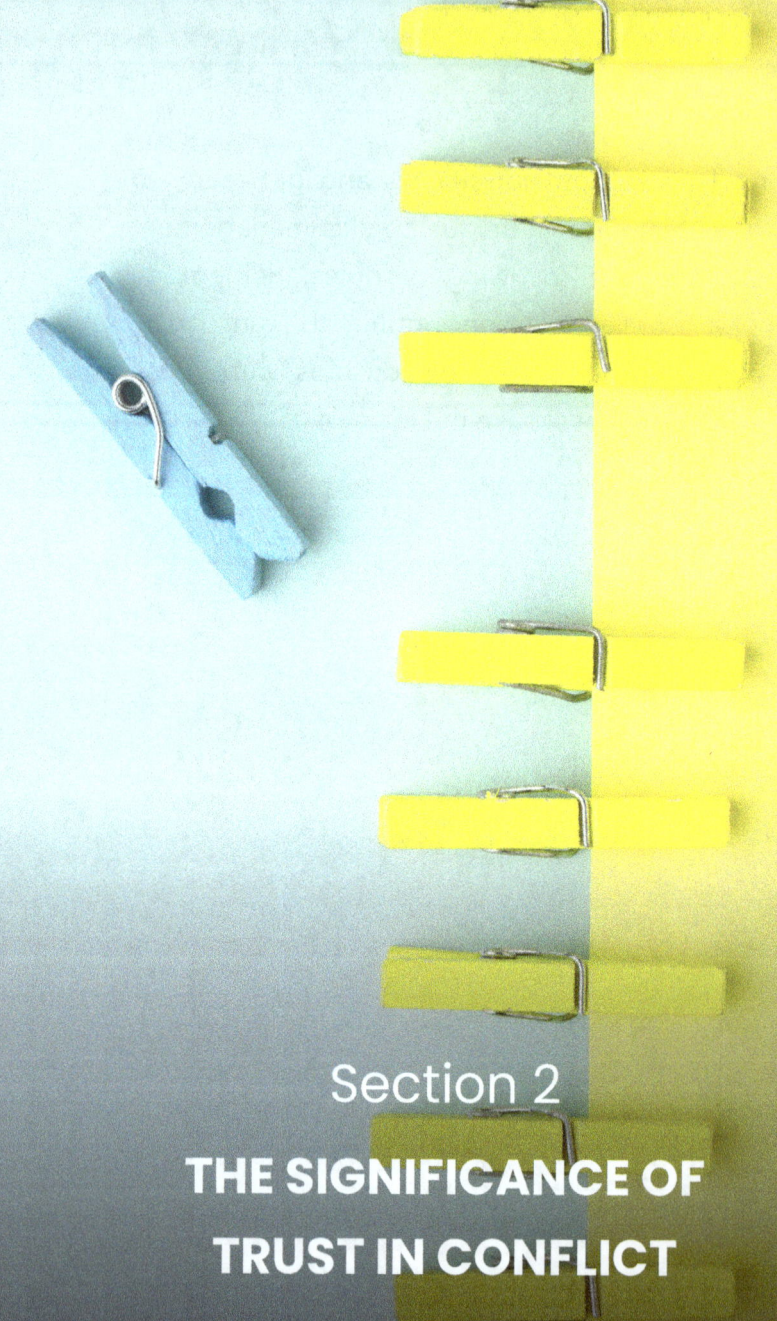

Section 2

**THE SIGNIFICANCE OF
TRUST IN CONFLICT**

Trust is like the heart and soul of navigating conflict–it's the unsung hero that wields tremendous influence on how we handle disagreements. In this section, we're diving deep into the essence of trust in conflict and why it's the secret sauce for unlocking positive outcomes. Let's unlock the power of trust and explore how it breathes life into effective communication, collaboration, and resolution in the midst of conflict.

Trust: The Bedrock of Thriving Relationships

Trust forms the bedrock of all our relationships, especially when the storm clouds of conflict gather. Picture it as a sturdy bridge connecting people–built on belief, reliability, and the art of keeping secrets. When trust graces our interactions, conflicts find their way into open and honest conversations, seeking resolution like old friends. But without trust, those storm clouds rumble louder, relationships tremble, and the road to resolution becomes an uphill battle.

Harmony in Trust and Communication

Trust and communication–like an inseparable duo, they dance their way through the ballroom of conflict. When trust takes the lead, communication follows with grace and poise. People feel free to speak their minds, unleashing thoughts, emotions, and concerns without a hint of trepidation. This trust-fueled communication waltzes its way into understanding, empathy, and collaborative problem-solving. However, when trust falters, the music stumbles, missteps ensue, and the dance of conflict veers off course.

Building Trust: The Art of Listening and Empathy

Ah, active listening and empathy–like a masterful duet that ignites trust's fiery spark. When trust takes center stage, ears perk up, and hearts lean in, genuinely seeking to grasp the beauty of others' perspectives. Empathy adds its flair, gracefully twirling into others' shoes, acknowledging their experiences with care and validation. Together, they create an ambiance of trust and camaraderie, making the conflict ballroom a safe haven for genuine connection.

Trust in Harmony with Collaboration

Collaborative conflict resolution—the grand finale of trust's symphony. In this spectacular act, trust is the conductor orchestrating a harmonious melody of collaboration. It's trust that unites individuals, inviting them to share ideas, information, and aspirations with unwavering confidence. Within this symphony of trust, collaboration sways with grace, embracing diverse perspectives that weave together enchanting resolutions to conflicts.

Trust Restored: Mend the Fences after Conflict's Storm

Sometimes, the winds of conflict blow fiercely, straining trust to its limits. But fear not, for trust is resilient. It's like a phoenix that rises from the ashes, ready to rebuild after the tempest has passed. Restoring trust is a grand masterpiece of honesty, remorse, and genuine action. Transparent communication, consistent follow-through, and keeping promises—all these brushstrokes paint a picture of renewed trust, breathing life back into strained relationships.

Trust as the Guardian of Conflict Prevention

Picture trust as a wise guardian, tirelessly watching over conflict's garden. It's not just there for the stormy days; it's also a proactive champion for conflict prevention. How? By planting seeds of fairness, transparency, and open dialogue in the soil of relationships. Embracing diverse perspectives and valuing the human tapestry—all these efforts nurture a positive conflict climate, where the seeds of destructive conflict struggle to take root.

Section 3

ART OF CONFLICT RESOLUTION

The art of conflict resolution is not solely about understanding your own personal conflict style or those of others. It also requires a set of key skills that underpin effective conflict resolution, such as communication, emotional intelligence, awareness of biases and assumptions, stress management techniques, and the understanding of apology and forgiveness in the context of resolving conflicts. Each of these elements serves as an important aspect of conflict resolution and strengthens your ability to manage conflicts successfully. Let's delve into each of these areas.

Communication Skills

Effective communication is the bedrock of conflict resolution. It involves expressing oneself clearly and assertively, truly listening to others, and being aware of non- verbal cues.

Clear and Assertive Expression: Clear communication involves being direct, honest, and respectful. Assertiveness, on the other hand, is about expressing your thoughts, feelings, and needs in an open way without violating the rights of others. It is a balance between aggression and passivity.

Active Listening: This skill requires giving your full attention to the speaker, reflecting back what you hear, and clarifying any points of confusion. It's about understanding, not just hearing.

Non-Verbal Cues: These include facial expressions, body language, and tone of voice. They can communicate just as much, if not more, than words.

Questions to ponder: How do you usually communicate during conflicts? What elements of your communication could you improve?

Emotional Intelligence

Emotional intelligence is the ability to recognize, understand, and manage our own emotions, as well as the ability to recognize, understand, and influence the emotions of others. In the context of conflict resolution, high emotional intelligence can facilitate a deeper understanding of the emotional landscape of a conflict, providing insight into the feelings and needs of all parties involved.

Questions to ponder: How aware are you of your emotions during conflicts? How well do you understand the emotions of others during a disagreement?

Bias and Assumptions

Everyone carries unconscious biases and assumptions, which can cloud our judgment and influence our reactions during conflicts. Recognizing and challenging these biases can pave the way for more fair and effective conflict resolution. It helps us to question our automatic reactions and assumptions, enabling us to respond more thoughtfully and constructively.

Questions to ponder: Can you identify any biases or assumptions that have influenced your approach to conflict in the past? How might you challenge these biases in the future?

Stress Management Techniques

Conflict can be stressful. Having a repertoire of stress management techniques can help prevent emotions from escalating and derailing conflict resolution efforts.

Techniques might include mindfulness practices, breathing exercises, or knowing when to take a break from a heated situation.

Questions to ponder: How do you usually handle stress during conflicts? Could any new stress management techniques be useful to you?

The Importance of Apology and Forgiveness in Conflict Resolution

Understanding when and how to apologize, and the role of forgiveness in conflict resolution, are crucial for repairing relationships post-conflict. An apology can validate the other person's feelings, while forgiveness can facilitate the release of resentment and the healing of emotional wounds.

Questions to ponder: How comfortable are you with apologizing during conflicts? How do you approach forgiveness after a conflict has been resolved?

By taking the time to understand and develop these skills, you will be better equipped to navigate the challenging terrain of conflict resolution. Remember, conflict is not just about disagreement, but also about growth and understanding.

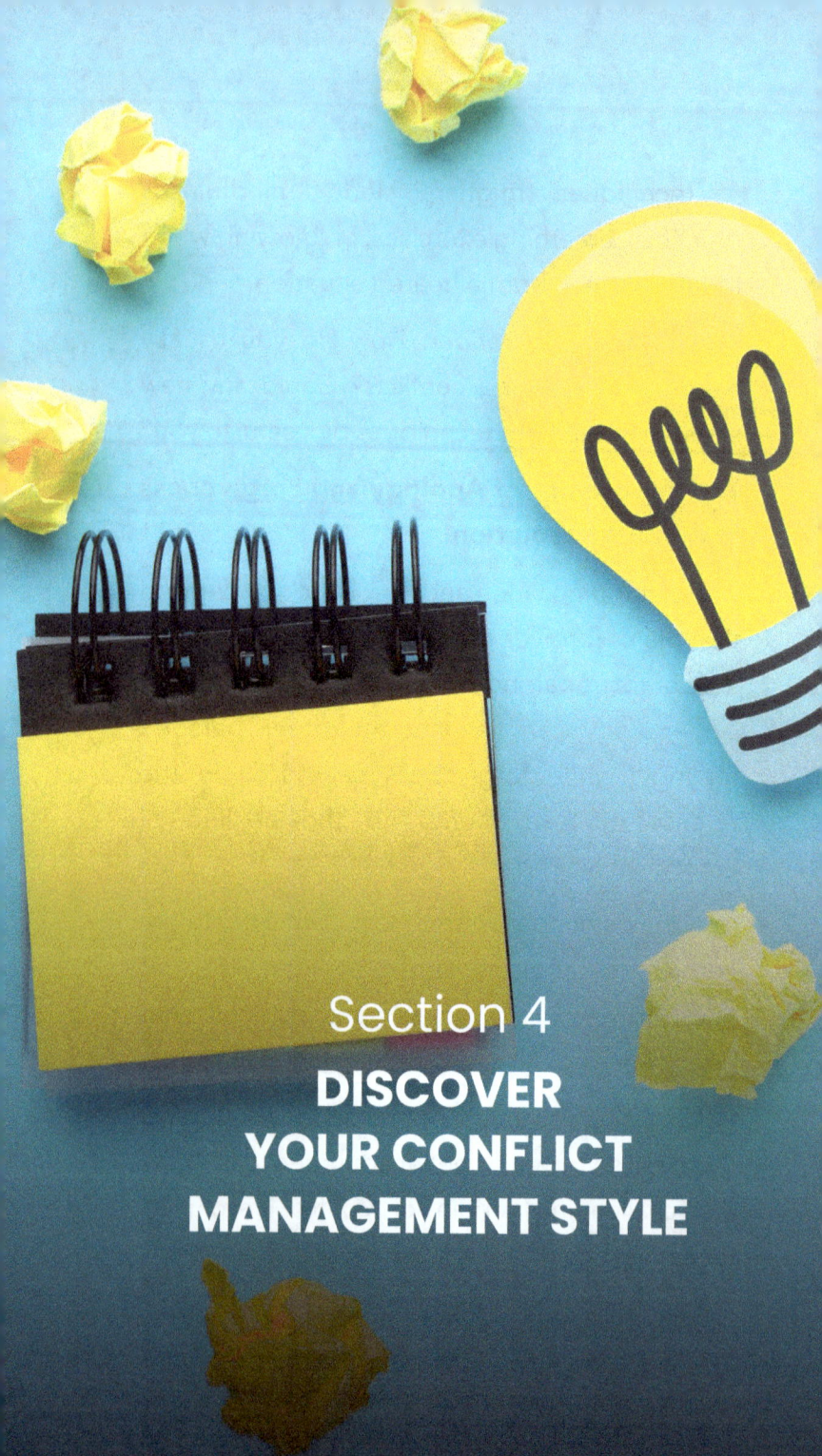

Section 4

**DISCOVER
YOUR CONFLICT
MANAGEMENT STYLE**

It's time to roll up our sleeves and dive into the nitty-gritty of some different conflict management styles. Like most things regarding leadership, there isn't a one-size- fits-all approach to managing conflict. "Leadership is the *art* of mobilizing others to want to struggle for shared aspirations." –James Kouzes and Barry Posner [emphasis added]. Different situations require different responses, and that is part of what makes this an art. It's like choosing the right pair of socks for the occasion: gym socks for a workout, dress socks for a board meeting, and, if you're feeling particularly adventurous, maybe even those Christmas socks with the reindeer on them for your next holiday party.

So, without further ado, here are the five common conflict management styles:

1. **Stepping Back**: This style is about distancing yourself from the thick of the conflict. Sometimes, it's like pressing the 'pause' button on a tense scene in a movie. You're not running away; just taking a breather. But remember, while it's a cool move when things are superheated, overuse can make you seem like a ghost, always disappearing when disagreements arise.

- *Pros*: This approach can help cool down heated situations and prevent minor issues from blowing out of proportion. It allows for more time to gather thoughts and consider responses.

- *Cons*: If overused, it can lead to unresolved issues piling up, which can create bigger problems down the line. It can also make you seem unengaged or indifferent, affecting your relationships with others.

2. **Taking the Lead**: You're the one who's not afraid to stand up and say, "I've got this!" You hold your ground, assert your opinions, and lead the charge. It's like being the superhero in a comic book, fighting for what you believe is right. But keep in mind; even superheroes need sidekicks. Don't forget to listen to others and consider their views.

   - *Pros*: This style can be effective when quick, decisive action is needed. It shows your commitment and conviction, which can inspire respect from others.

- *Cons*: If you always insist on your way, it can make others feel unheard or undervalued. This style can also escalate conflicts if not tempered with empathy and listening.

3. **Harmonizing**: You're the peacekeeper who smooths the ruffled feathers and says, "Let's all get along." You're willing to put others' needs and views before your own to maintain harmony. It's like you're conducting a choir, ensuring all the voices blend beautifully. Just remember, your voice is important too. Don't let it get lost in the chorus.

- *Pros*: It can help maintain relationships and team harmony. This approach can be especially effective when the issue is more important to the other party.

- *Cons*: Constantly yielding to others can lead to your needs and concerns being overlooked. It might also encourage others to take advantage of your accommodating nature.

4. **Balancing**: You're the master of the middle ground, finding a spot where everyone's somewhat satisfied. It's like being a tightrope walker, carefully maintaining balance to keep everyone from falling. But remember, sometimes the middle ground isn't the best. Don't be afraid to push for more when it's needed.

    - *Pros*: This style can lead to quick resolutions and maintain relationships by ensuring everyone's needs are somewhat met. It shows your flexibility and willingness to meet others halfway.

    - *Cons*: Compromises may not fully satisfy anyone involved and can lead to sub- optimal solutions. Over-reliance on this style can discourage thinking outside the box and finding innovative solutions.

5. **Team Building**: You're the one who says, "Two heads are better than one." You believe in creating solutions that fully satisfy everyone involved. It's like assembling a puzzle, ensuring every piece fits perfectly.

But keep in mind not every situation needs a complex solution. Sometimes, a simpler approach might be more effective.

- *Pros*: This style can lead to high-quality solutions that fully address everyone's concerns. It fosters a sense of ownership and commitment among all parties involved.

- *Cons*: It can be time-consuming and impractical for all situations, especially when quick decisions are needed. It also requires high trust and open communication, which might not always be present.

Before you start labeling yourself, remember that no style is inherently "good" or "bad." It's all about choosing the right tool for the job. And sometimes, it's about realizing that the tool you've been using all along might not be the best fit for every situation.

So, what's your go-to style when conflict arises? Don't worry; there's no need to answer that right away. We've got a little self-assessment coming up next that will help you figure it out.

Section 5

SELF–ASSESSMENT –
UNCOVER YOUR CONFLICT
RESOLUTION STYLE

Buckle up because we're about to take off on a journey of self-discovery, and let's dive into your unique approach to conflict resolution. Remember, there's no 'bad' or 'wrong' here. It's all about understanding your style and learning when to flex it or switch it up.

Before you dive into these scenarios, grab a scratch piece of paper, or open a new note on your device. As you go through each scenario, jot down the response that feels most like your go-to approach. Don't overthink it – this isn't a high school exam, and there's no teacher to impress! Just let your instincts guide you. Writing down your answers will help you keep track and reflect on your conflict management style more effectively.

1. **Scenario:** You and a team member have different ideas about how to execute a project.

A) You step back and let their idea take the lead.

B) You try convincing them that your idea is superior.

C) You suggest a blend of both ideas, even if it's not ideal.

D) You strive to create a new solution that satisfies both of you.

E) You avoid the conversation and decide to discuss it later.

2. Scenario: A colleague frequently interrupts you during meetings.

A) You don't confront them and wait for the right moment to bring it up.

B) You assertively tell them that their behavior is not acceptable.

C) You ask them to let you finish speaking but also try to speed up your delivery.

D) You have a one-on-one discussion to find a mutual understanding of communication during meetings.

E) You choose to ignore it to avoid an awkward situation.

3. Scenario: A team member consistently misses deadlines, affecting the overall project timeline.

A) You decide not to confront them, hoping they'll improve their performance over time.

B) You firmly explain the importance of meeting deadlines and the consequences of not doing so.

C) You propose adjusting some of their tasks to relieve them, even if it means more work for you or others.

D) You engage in a discussion to understand their challenges and work on a mutually agreeable solution.

E) You accommodate their pace, adjusting the project timeline instead of confronting them.

4. Scenario: Two of your team members are in conflict, and it's affecting the team's morale.

A) You choose not to intervene directly, hoping they'll resolve the issue independently.

B) You assertively intervene and dictate a solution based on your viewpoint.

C) You suggest a compromise that might not fully satisfy either party but will calm the situation.

D) You facilitate a conversation between them, aiming for a resolution that addresses both their concerns.

E) You take a step back and let them decide the course of action, even if it affects the team's morale.

5. Scenario: You receive feedback from your superior that you don't completely agree with.

A) You don't challenge the feedback, instead choosing to reflect on it later.

B) You assertively express your disagreement and provide your perspective.

C) You partially agree with the feedback to maintain a positive relationship with your superior.

D) You engage in a discussion to understand their perspective and express your own, aiming for a mutual understanding.

E) You accept the feedback graciously, putting your superior's perspective above your own.

6. Scenario: During a team brainstorming session, your idea is criticized.

A) You don't defend your idea, deciding to contribute another one instead.

B) You defend your idea and argue its merits.

C) You suggest modifying your idea to address the criticisms.

D) You propose a session to refine the idea together, incorporating everyone's feedback.

E) You withdraw your idea and support the one that's being favored by others.

After reviewing these scenarios, tally up your responses to uncover your primary conflict resolution style!

There isn't a right or wrong style. All of the styles have pros and cons to them. This exercise is about growing in awareness and understanding, equipping you with a foundation to build upon as you journey into the world of conflict resolution. Next, we'll delve deeper into each style, offering insights and strategies to navigate the choppy waters of conflict

Section 6

WHAT'S YOUR STYLE?

Alright, let's break down what your answers might say about your go-to style when the heat is on:

If you're picking mostly **A's**, you're a bit of a "**Step Back**" type of person. You're the master of the strategic retreat, often choosing to sidestep the conflict or put it on the back burner.

Now, if you're all about those **B's**, you're rocking the "**Take the Lead**" style. You're not afraid to stand your ground and put your needs and concerns front and center.

If **C's** are your jam, you're a "**Balancer**" at heart. You're all about finding that sweet spot in the middle, juggling your needs with those of others.

If you chose mostly **D's**, you're a "**Team Builder**." You're seeking that win-win situation, listening to everyone's concerns and working towards a solution that benefits the whole team.

And if **E's** are your go-to, you're a "**Harmonizer**." You're often willing to put others' needs and concerns first to keep the peace.

But remember, this isn't about sticking a label on you and calling it a day. It's about understanding your natural instincts when you're in the thick of it. The real goal is to become a conflict chameleon, adapting your style to different situations and relationships.

Section 7

EMOTIONAL INTELLIGENCE IN CONFLICT RESOLUTION

Before we jump into the nitty-gritty of emotional intelligence (or EQ for short), let's break it down in simple terms. Imagine EQ as your social radar, your ability to read the room. It's like having an internal emotional GPS that helps you navigate not just your feelings but also those of the people around you. It's about being tuned in to the emotional channel - knowing when to turn up the empathy, when to dial down the drama, and when to recalibrate your responses based on how others are feeling.

Think of it as your emotional toolkit. You've got tools for understanding and managing your own emotions (no more getting blindsided by a sudden bout of anger in the middle of a meeting), and tools for reading and responding to the emotions of others (like knowing just the right thing to say to a team member who's feeling overwhelmed). This isn't about being touchy-feely or a mind reader; it's about being smart with emotions – yours and others'. And in the world of conflict resolution, that's a superpower worth having!

Daniel Goleman said, "There is an old-fashioned word for the body of skills that emotional intelligence represents: character." The bullets below provide some specific tactics and strategies for using EQ when managing different types of conflict:

- Recognizing and managing your own emotions.

- Acknowledging and Validating the emotions of others.

- Listening with the intent to understand the other party's perspective.

- Promoting a positive emotional climate.

- Focusing on interests, not positions.

- Letting go of the desire to be right.

- Encouraging a solutions-oriented mindset.

Understanding EQ and Conflict

EQ is your secret superpower when dealing with conflict. You can recognize, understand, and manage your emotions and those of others. This awareness can help you navigate and control the emotional landscape of a conflict situation, leading to more effective and satisfying resolutions.

EQ vs. IQ vs. Personality: The Crucial Differences

It's important to distinguish EQ from other aspects of your mental landscape. IQ, or cognitive intelligence, refers to your ability to learn and process information. It remains largely unchanged throughout your life. Your personality, on the other hand, is your stable set of characteristics, such as your preference for introversion or extroversion.

EQ differs from both in that it is a flexible skill that can be developed and improved over time. It's about emotional learning and growth, not static states or fixed capacities. So, no matter your current EQ level, there's always room for enhancement!

The Importance of EQ in Conflict Resolution

EQ is a powerful tool when dealing with conflicts. It enables you to recognize the emotional underpinnings of conflicts, spot your emotional triggers, and manage your reactions. A high EQ allows you to remain calm and collected during heated moments and to understand and empathize with the other party's emotions. This understanding can transform conflict from a roadblock into a path toward deeper understanding and stronger relationships.

Boosting Your EQ for Better Conflict Management

The best part about EQ is that it's a flexible skill that can be enhanced. With consistent practice, you can increase your EQ and reap the benefits in your personal and professional life, including more effective conflict resolution. It's akin to learning to dance: with each step you practice, you become more adept, eventually waltzing your way through the dance floor of life with grace and ease.

Section 8

CULTURAL CONSIDERATIONS

In an increasingly connected world, cultural understanding is crucial to conflict resolution. Different cultures have different perspectives, norms, and expectations regarding conflict and its solution. Ignoring these differences can lead to misunderstandings and escalate conflicts while acknowledging and respecting them can facilitate dialogue and compromise. Here are some points to consider when dealing with conflict across cultures:

- Understand cultural norms while avoiding stereotyping.

- Recognize that dealmaking across cultures can result in more challenging negotiations.

- Use negotiation skills and techniques to avoid cognitive biases at the bargaining table.

The Role of Culture in Conflict

Culture can significantly influence how we perceive and approach conflict. It shapes our communication styles, values, and conflict-resolution strategies. Understanding these cultural differences can resolve conflicts in a diverse environment.

Communication Styles Across Cultures

Different cultures have different communication styles, which can sometimes lead to misunderstandings. Some cultures favor direct communication, while others prefer a more indirect, subtle approach. Recognizing these differences can help prevent miscommunication and ease conflict resolution.

Cultural Values and Conflict

Cultural values can also play a significant role in conflicts. For example, some cultures prioritize harmony and group consensus, while others value individual assertiveness and competition. Understanding these values can help provide context for a person's behavior during a conflict and can guide the resolution process.

Cultural Sensitivity in Conflict Resolution

To effectively resolve conflicts in a diverse environment, it's important to practice cultural sensitivity. This involves respecting cultural differences, avoiding stereotypes, and understanding the cultural contexts of the other parties involved in the conflict.

Developing Cultural Intelligence (CQ) for Conflict Management

Cultural Intelligence, or CQ, is the capability to function effectively in culturally diverse situations. By developing your CQ, you can better navigate and resolve conflicts in a multicultural context. Like EQ, CQ is a skill that can be learned and improved over time.

Remember, understanding and respecting cultural differences is not about reinforcing stereotypes but acknowledging the richness and diversity of human experience and using this understanding to communicate and resolve conflicts more efficiently. Combining Emotional Intelligence with Cultural Intelligence allows you to navigate even the most complex conflict situations with wisdom and skill.

Section 9

MEDIATION SKILLS FOR CONFLICT RESOLUTION

Mediation is a common method of conflict resolution that involves a neutral third party - the mediator - who helps the conflicting parties to communicate, negotiate, and reach a mutually acceptable solution. Now, let's be real: in the workplace, finding a mediator who's as neutral as Switzerland might be a tall order. Often, the mediator is someone from within the team or organization, and that's where things get tricky. Let's unpack some common pitfalls and how to sidestep them:

Common Pitfalls and How to Avoid Them:

1. **Accidental Bias**: It's easy to lean towards the opinions of those we know better or agree with. To combat this, consciously remind yourself to weigh each side's arguments equally. Remind yourself that your role is not to take sides but to facilitate a fair resolution.

2. **Staying Objective**: Keep your personal opinions and experiences out of the discussion. Focus on the facts and the feelings expressed by the parties involved. If you find your own biases creeping in, take a moment to step back and reset.

3. **Talking Stick Method**: Remember the old 'talking stick' concept? Use it metaphorically. Only the person with the 'stick' speaks, ensuring everyone gets a chance to voice their thoughts without interruption. This method helps keep the mediation structured and fair.

4. **Listening More, Talking Less**: As a mediator, your job is more about listening than talking. Guide the conversation, ask clarifying questions, and then step back. Let the parties involved express themselves. Sometimes, all it takes to resolve a conflict is for everyone to feel heard.

Understanding Mediation Now that we've covered what to watch out for, let's delve into understanding mediation itself. Mediation is a process where an unbiased (as far as possible) third party, the mediator, helps those in conflict to communicate and negotiate to reach a mutually acceptable resolution. The mediator doesn't solve the problem but helps everyone else figure it out. It's less about being the hero and more about being a top-notch guide.

Role of a Mediator As a mediator, think of yourself as a facilitator. Your job is to clarify misunderstandings and help everyone involved find their path to resolution. It's like being a lighthouse, guiding ships through foggy waters.

The following points outline key mediation skills and techniques:

- Make Multiple Equivalent Simultaneous Offers (MESOs) to create value in dealmaking.

- Use joint fact-finding to help disputants reach agreement.

- Use negotiation games to assess risks of escalating conflict.

Understanding Mediation

Mediation is a process where an unbiassed third party, the mediator, helps those in conflict to communicate and negotiate to reach a mutually acceptable resolution.

The mediator does not impose a solution but facilitates the conversation and negotiation between the parties.

Role of a Mediator

As a mediator, your role is not to judge, take sides, or provide solutions. Instead, you facilitate communication, help clarify misunderstandings, and guide parties towards their own resolution. You're like a guide, helping the parties navigate the complex terrain of conflict towards a place of understanding and resolution.

Key Mediation Skills

- **Active Listening:** This involves not just hearing, but truly understanding and reflecting the perspectives and feelings of the parties involved.

- **Questioning:** Asking open-ended and probing questions to explore the issues more deeply and reveal underlying needs and interests.

- **Reframing:** This involves restating negative or inflammatory statements in a neutral or positive way to shift perspectives and reduce tensions.

- **Building Rapport:** Establishing trust and understanding with all parties to foster open and honest communication.

- **Problem-Solving:** Guiding the parties in exploring options and creating mutually beneficial solutions.

Stages of Mediation

- **Introduction:** Setting the ground rules and explaining the mediation process.

- **Story-Telling:** Each party shares their perspective and experience of the conflict.

- **Issue Identification:** Clarifying and prioritizing the issues that need to be resolved.

- **Problem-Solving:** Exploring options and negotiating a mutually acceptable resolution.

- **Agreement:** Documenting the resolution in a written agreement that outlines the future actions of each party.

Mediation in Action

Mediation can be applied in various settings, from workplace disputes to international conflicts. It is a powerful tool for conflict resolution that empowers the parties involved to create their own solutions, rather than imposing a one- size-fits-all solution.

By enhancing your mediation skills, you can become a more effective conflict resolver, helping others navigate through their conflicts towards understanding and resolution. Up next, we'll explore more advanced concepts and techniques for effective conflict resolution. Stay tuned!

Section 10:

ADVANCED CONCEPTS AND TECHNIQUES FOR EFFECTIVE CONFLICT RESOLUTION

As with any field, there are advanced skills in conflict resolution that can be particularly effective in complex or challenging situations. These skills often require a deep understanding of conflict dynamics, strong communication abilities, and the capacity to think strategically and creatively about solutions. Let's dive into some of these advanced conflict resolution skills, but this time, we'll pair each concept with a practical example or exercise to help you grasp and apply these techniques in real-life situations.

- Use the "Mitchell Principles" (commitments to open communication, non- violence, and democracy) to facilitate negotiation.

- Utilize techniques for resolving conflicts within the family.

- Apply negotiation strategies for dealing with difficult situations with children.

- Understand that each conflict has unique aspects and requires a unique approach for resolution.

1. The Iceberg Theory

The Iceberg Theory suggests that much like an iceberg, only a small portion of a conflict is visible above the surface (the issue that is explicitly stated), while the bulk of it lies beneath (the underlying emotions, past experiences, unexpressed needs). Navigating conflict effectively often involves exploring what's beneath the surface to address the root cause of the conflict.

Example: In your next conflict, try to identify what's 'below the surface.' Ask questions like, "What past experiences might be influencing my/their feelings about this issue?" This deeper understanding can help you address the root cause of the conflict, not just the visible symptoms.

2. BATNA (Best Alternative To a Negotiated Agreement)

BATNA is a concept from negotiation theory that represents the best outcome you can achieve if you fail to reach an agreement in the current negotiation.

Understanding your BATNA empowers you to negotiate from a position of strength, knowing when to compromise and when to walk away.

Exercise: Think of a current conflict and identify your BATNA. What is the best outcome you can achieve if the negotiation fails? Understanding this will give you clarity on when to compromise and when to stand firm.

3. Transformative Mediation

This is a type of mediation that focuses on empowering and recognizing the parties involved in the conflict. The aim is not just to resolve the conflict, but also to foster personal growth and transformation through the process.

Practice: In your next mediation role, focus on recognizing and reinforcing the strengths of each party. Encourage them to see the conflict as an opportunity for personal and relational growth.

4. Conflict Mapping

Conflict mapping involves visually diagramming the elements of a conflict: the parties involved, their positions, underlying interests, power dynamics, and the context. This helps to clarify the complexity of the conflict and identify potential avenues for resolution.

Activity: Draw a conflict map for a current dispute. Include the parties involved, their positions, underlying interests, power dynamics, and the context. This can help identify potential solutions.

5. Reframing Positions as Interests

Parties in conflict often focus on their positions (what they want) rather than their interests (why they want it). By reframing positions as interests, you can uncover common ground and create win-win solutions that address the underlying needs and desires of all parties.

Scenario Practice: In a disagreement, instead of arguing for your position, try to express the underlying interests. Ask the other party to do the same and look for common ground.

6. Psychological Safety

Creating a space where parties feel safe to express their thoughts, feelings, and needs without fear of judgment or retaliation is critical for effective conflict resolution. This involves setting ground rules, demonstrating respect and empathy, and promoting open and honest communication.

Technique: Next time you're in a conflict, set ground rules for respectful communication, demonstrate empathy, and encourage openness. Pay attention to how this changes the dynamics of the discussion.

7. Facilitative vs. Evaluative Mediation

Facilitative mediators guide the process and help parties find their own solutions, while evaluative mediators offer their own insights and suggestions for resolution. Both approaches have their pros and cons and may be more or less suitable depending on the specific context of the conflict.

Example for Facilitative Mediation: Imagine you're mediating a dispute between two departments over budget allocations. Instead of suggesting a solution, you help them articulate their needs, concerns, and priorities, facilitating a dialogue that leads them to their own mutually agreeable solution.

Example for Evaluative Mediation: Now, consider a scenario where you're mediating a contract dispute between a supplier and your company. Here, you might use your expertise to assess the situation and suggest a compromise based on industry standards and legal precedents.

Applying these Techniques: Knowing which style to use is crucial. In situations where maintaining relationships is key, and parties are capable of finding solutions themselves, facilitative mediation works best. But when a conflict involves technical details or legal issues where your expertise is valuable, evaluative mediation might be more appropriate.

By integrating these advanced concepts and techniques into your conflict resolution toolkit, you can enhance your ability to navigate and resolve complex conflicts effectively.

Section 11

STRATEGIES AND TECHNIQUES

"A good manager doesn't try to eliminate conflict; he tries to keep it from wasting the energies of his people. If you're the boss and your people fight you openly when they think that you are wrong--that's healthy."

- Robert Townsend

1. Acknowledging and Validating

This one's a personal favorite of mine, called "Acknowledging and Validating." It's like the Swiss Army knife of conflict management strategies. So, let's break it down.

Acknowledging

Acknowledging is about letting the other person know they've been heard and what they're saying matters. It's like saying, "I listened, I heard, and I cared." It's not just about parroting back what they said but showing that you really get it.

For example, Let's say a colleague tells you, "I've been working late every night this week. I'm exhausted, and it feels like no one even notices." An acknowledging response could be, "It sounds really tough, working late every night and feeling like your efforts are going unnoticed. "

Remember, when you're acknowledging, it's not about you. It's about the other person. So, keep the focus on their feelings and experiences.

Validating

Now, let's move on to validating. This is where you let the other person know their feelings are normal and understandable. It's not about agreeing with them but showing empathy and not judging.

For example, imagine a friend shares, "I'm really nervous about this presentation tomorrow. I'm worried I'm going to mess it up." A validating response might be, "It's completely normal to feel nervous before a big presentation. You're putting yourself out there, and it's natural to worry about how it will go."

The Acknowledge-Validate-Question Cycle

Now, let's see how this works in a conversation. Suppose your teammate says, "I'm feeling overwhelmed with this project. There's so much to do, and I don't know where to start."

First, you acknowledge: "It sounds like this project is really stressing you out, with so much to do and not knowing where to begin."

Then, you validate: "It's totally normal to feel overwhelmed when facing a big project. It can be daunting when there's a lot to tackle."

Finally, you ask a question to keep the conversation going: "What's one small part of the project you feel confident you could start with?"

And then, you repeat the cycle as the conversation continues. This approach helps the other person feel heard and understood and keeps the conversation constructive and focused on solutions.

2. **Active Listening:** Another powerful tool in resolving conflict is to simply listen. Active listening involves not just hearing the other person's words but seeking to understand their perspective and feelings. It's about making the other person feel heard and valued. This can help to de-escalate tensions and open up a space for constructive dialogue. Remember, listening doesn't

mean you agree with the other person, but it does show respect for their viewpoint.

3. **Effective Communication:** Clear, open, and honest communication is essential in resolving conflicts. This involves expressing your feelings and needs in a straightforward, non-accusatory way. Using "I" statements (e.g., "I feel upset when...") rather than "you" statements (e.g., "You always...") can help prevent the other person from becoming defensive.

4. **Emotional Intelligence:** Understanding and managing your own emotions, as well as empathizing with others, can greatly aid in conflict resolution. You can help keep the situation from escalating by staying calm and composed. Empathizing with the other person can also help you understand their viewpoint and find a mutually satisfactory resolution.

5. **Problem-Solving Approach:** Instead of focusing on who's right or wrong, try to approach the conflict as a problem to be solved together. Think about it like, "How do *we* solve this?" This involves identifying all

parties' underlying needs and concerns and finding a solution that addresses them. This collaborative approach can lead to more satisfying and long-lasting resolutions.

6. **Respect for Differences:** Recognizing and respecting that people have different perspectives and ways of doing things can help prevent and manage conflicts. Differences can actually be a source of strength and innovation if managed properly. It's about finding a way to harness these differences in a positive way.

7. **Seeking Help:** If a conflict is too difficult to resolve on your own, don't hesitate to seek help. This could be a superior, a trusted colleague, or a professional mediator. An outside perspective can often help to break the deadlock and find a solution.

8. **Practicing Patience:** Conflict resolution is often not a quick process. It takes time to fully understand the other person's perspective and to find a solution that satisfies everyone. Being patient and not rushing the process can lead to better outcomes.

Remember, the goal of conflict resolution isn't to 'win' the argument but to find a solution that respects everyone's needs and preserves relationships. It's about turning a potentially negative situation into an opportunity for growth and learning. So, next time you find yourself in a conflict, take a deep breath, keep these strategies in mind, and dive in.

Section 12

INDIVIDUAL EXERCISES

Now, we're moving into the "Individual Exercises" section. This is your personal training ground, your dojo if you will. Here, you'll find a series of exercises designed to help you flex those conflict management muscles. Don't worry, there's no heavy lifting involved, just some thoughtful reflection and self-assessment. So, get ready to break a mental sweat and let's start training!

Exercise 1: Reflective Journal

A reflective journal is a personal tool that can help individuals track their progress, note their thoughts, and build self-awareness about their conflict resolution skills.

- **Content:** The journal entries should include a description of the conflict situation, the individual's initial reaction, the conflict style they used, the outcome, and their reflections on how they handled it. They can also write about their feelings and thoughts during the conflict and how it affected their relationship with the other party.

- **Instructions:** Users should be encouraged to write in their journal regularly, ideally after every significant conflict they experience. This could be a disagreement with a co-worker, a dispute with a family member, or even a minor disagreement with a stranger. The aim is to make regular self-reflection a habit.

- **Goals:** The goal of the journal is to increase self-awareness and gain insight into one's own behavior and reactions in conflict situations. Over time, users should be able to identify patterns in their behavior, understand their strengths and weaknesses in conflict resolution, and use this knowledge to improve their skills.

Exercise 2: Conflict Style Self-Assessment

In this exercise, the individual will reflect on a past conflict they have experienced and try to identify the conflict style they used in that situation.

- **Instructions:** Think about a recent conflict you were involved in. It could be anything from a disagreement with a coworker, to a dispute with a family member or friend. Reflect on how you handled the situation and determine which conflict style you used. Write down the details of the conflict and your analysis in your reflective journal.

- **Goal:** This exercise will help individuals develop self-awareness about their default conflict styles and consider how they might use different strategies in the future.

Exercise 3: Role-Play with a Friend

If you have a friend or family member who's also interested in improving their conflict resolution skills, this exercise can be a fun and insightful way to learn.

- **Instructions:** Each of you should come up with a fictional conflict scenario and role-play it. After the role-play, discuss the conflict styles you each used, the strategies you employed, and how you felt during the conflict. You can then switch roles and repeat the exercise.

- **Goal:** This exercise will provide an opportunity to practice conflict resolution skills in a safe environment. It will also provide insight into how others might perceive your conflict resolution style.

Section 13

GROUP EXERCISES

Interactive Exercise 1: "The Conflict Carousel"

This exercise can be done in small groups or pairs. Each group will receive a set of conflict scenarios (you can use real-life examples or hypothetical situations). The task for each group is to identify the conflict style best suited to handle each situation, discuss why they chose that style, and outline a potential resolutionstrategy. After a set time limit, groups rotate scenarios, giving participants exposure to a range of conflicts and resolution strategies.

Purpose: This exercise helps participants understand the different conflict styles in action and their suitability for various situations. It also promotes discussion and collaboration.

Scenarios

Scenario 1: Deadline Disputes

Your team has a project due in one week, and you're behind schedule. Two team members, Alex and Sam, are arguing about how to proceed. Alex believes that the team should put in extra hours to ensure the project is completed on time, while Sam insists on asking for an extension.

Conflict Style: Balancer

In this scenario, the Balancer style is most appropriate because the situation calls for a collaborative effort to reach a solution that satisfies both parties. The team needs to find a way to complete the project on time without overworking.

Resolution Strategy:

The team could devise a plan where they split the remaining tasks equally, work on them concurrently, and put in a few extra hours if needed. They could also draft a backup plan to request an extension, presenting their progress and the challenges they faced, just in case their efforts to complete the project on time fall short.

Scenario 2: Office Space Allocation

There's a dispute between the marketing and sales teams over who gets the newly available office space. The sales team insists they need it for client meetings, while the marketing team argues it's essential for their creative brainstorming sessions.

Conflict Style: Team Builder

In this scenario, the Team Builder style is most appropriate because it's unlikely that one team will completely give way to the other. Both teams have valid reasons for needing the space.

Resolution Strategy:

A possible solution could be to create a schedule where both teams share the space, using it at different times or on different days. This way, both teams' needs are met, and the space is utilized effectively.

These scenarios can be used as a starting point for the "Conflict Carousel" exercise. Participants can discuss the situations, identify the conflict styles, and come up with their own resolution strategies.

Interactive Exercise 2: "Solution Sculpture"

This is a role-play exercise where each participant takes turns playing the role of a conflict mediator. The group is given a scenario, and the mediator must use the strategies discussed in the course to guide the parties towards a resolution. The rest of the group observes and then provides feedback.

Purpose: This exercise allows participants to practice their conflict resolution skills in a supportive, feedback-rich environment.

Scenario 1: Role-Play a Conflict Resolution

You're a manager at a retail store, and one of your employees, Jordan, is frequently getting into disputes with customers. Jordan is great at their job but tends to be defensive when customers raise issues or complaints.

Conflict Style: Harmonizer

In this case, the Harmonizer style might be the best initial approach. As a manager, you understand that Jordan's intention isn't to create conflict, but their defensive nature might escalate situations unnecessarily. By accommodating the customers' needs, you can keep the situation under control while you address the issue with Jordan.

Resolution Strategy:

You could role-play scenarios with Jordan, helping them understand how their reactions may be perceived and coaching them to handle difficult customers more effectively. Regular feedback and training sessions could also be beneficial.

Scenario 2: Conflict Over Office Space

You're a team leader in an open office environment. Two of your team members, Alex and Jamie, are in conflict over the seating arrangement. Alex prefers sitting near the window for natural light, but Jamie complains that the sunlight on their computer screen makes it hard to work.

Conflict Style: Balancer

This scenario calls for a Balancer style. Both parties have valid concerns and it would be fair to find a middle ground that suits them both.

Resolution Strategy:

You could arrange a discussion between Alex and Jamie and suggest a possible compromise. Perhaps Alex could use a desk lamp for natural light, or they could switch desks at a certain time of day to balance their needs. This role-play would help participants understand how to achieve compromise in a practical situation.

Interactive Exercise 3: "Conflict Improv"

In this activity, participants form pairs. One person in each pair receives a card with a conflict style and a brief scenario. They must then initiate a conflict with their partner, who does not know which style they're using. The partner has to identify the conflict style and respond effectively.

Purpose: This fun and engaging exercise helps reinforce knowledge of the conflict styles and encourages participants to think quickly and adapt their responses to different styles.

Remember, the key to these exercises is to create a safe, supportive environment where participants feel comfortable sharing their thoughts and ideas. Also, be sure to debrief thoroughly after each activity to ensure everyone understands the learnings and takeaways.

Negotiate a Win-Win Outcome

Scenario 1: Project Prioritization

You're a team leader, and two of your team members, Taylor and Morgan, are at odds over which project to prioritize. Taylor insists on focusing on Project A because it's closer to completion, while Morgan believes Project B, though more challenging, will have a bigger impact.

Conflict Style: Balancer

The Balancer style is fitting for this scenario, as it focuses on addressing the interests and concerns of both parties to reach a mutually beneficial solution.

Resolution Strategy:

You could arrange a meeting with Taylor and Morgan and facilitate a discussion where they each present their cases. By considering the pros and cons of each project, the team could arrive at a solution that might involve dividing resources between the two projects or finding a way to expedite Project A without neglecting Project B.

Scenario 2: Resource Allocation

You're managing a small team that's working on two important projects. There's a conflict between team members about how to allocate the limited resources. Half the team believes Project X needs more resources because of its complexity, while the other half insists that Project Y is more urgent.

Conflict Style: Balancer

The Balancer style is suitable for this scenario, as it would involve understanding the needs and constraints of both projects and finding a way to satisfy both parties.

Resolution Strategy:

You could facilitate a discussion where team members present their arguments and together develop a plan for resource allocation that considers both the complexity of Project X and the urgency of Project Y. This may involve creative problem-solving, such as bringing in additional temporary resources or finding ways to streamline tasks. The aim is to ensure both projects can progress effectively, showcasing a win-win negotiation.

Section 14

CASE STUDIES

Case Study 1: Overcoming Cultural Barriers

Case Study: Imagine you're leading a negotiation team in a multinational corporation. Your team is tasked with securing a crucial partnership with a company based in Japan. As you sit across the table from your Japanese counterparts, you notice subtle differences in communication styles and business etiquette. While you're used to direct and assertive negotiation tactics, your Japanese counterparts prefer a more indirect and relationship-focused approach. This cultural disconnect becomes evident as the negotiation progresses, leading to misunderstandings and tensions on both sides.

Explanation: In cross-cultural negotiations like this one, it's essential to recognize and navigate cultural differences effectively. Failure to do so can lead to breakdowns in communication and hinder the negotiation process. Understanding cultural norms and adapting your approach accordingly is crucial for building trust and reaching mutually beneficial agreements.

Key Takeaways: Leadership transcends borders, and effective negotiation across cultures requires cultural sensitivity and adaptability. Avoid relying on stereotypes and take the time to understand the cultural context of your counterparts. By demonstrating respect for cultural differences and adopting a collaborative mindset, you can overcome barriers and foster successful international partnerships.

Application: Next time you find yourself negotiating with individuals from a different cultural background, take proactive steps to educate yourself about their culture. Engage in cultural sensitivity training, conduct research on cultural norms and communication styles, and demonstrate genuine curiosity and respect for your counterparts' perspectives. By embracing diversity and cultural competence, you can enhance your negotiation skills and achieve positive outcomes in cross-cultural contexts.

Questions and Action:

1. Reflect on past experiences of negotiating across cultures. What challenges did you encounter, and how did you address them?

2. Consider how cultural differences impact negotiation dynamics in your workplace. What strategies can you implement to bridge cultural divides and promote effective communication?

3. Identify one concrete step you can take to enhance your cultural competence and improve your ability to navigate cross-cultural negotiations.

Case Study 2: Importance of Negotiation in Business

Case Study: Picture yourself as the manager of a small startup company seeking funding from potential investors. You're scheduled to meet with a group of venture capitalists to pitch your business idea and secure financial backing. As you prepare for the meeting, you anticipate tough questions and intense negotiations regarding equity, valuation, and terms of investment. Your goal is to strike a deal that aligns with your company's growth strategy while satisfying the investors' expectations for return on investment.

Explanation: In the high-stakes world of business negotiations, effective negotiation skills are essential for achieving favorable outcomes and driving organizational success. Whether you're negotiating funding deals, partnership agreements, or client contracts, the ability to advocate for your interests while finding common ground with stakeholders is critical. Negotiation skills enable you to navigate complex business scenarios, resolve conflicts, and capitalize on opportunities for growth and expansion.

Key Takeaways: Leadership in business requires mastery of negotiation techniques to navigate competitive landscapes and capitalize on strategic opportunities. By honing your negotiation skills, you can enhance your ability to influence outcomes, build strong relationships, and drive organizational success.

Application: Take proactive steps to develop and refine your negotiation skills through practice, training, and continuous learning. Seek out opportunities to negotiate in various business contexts, analyze negotiation outcomes, and identify areas for improvement.

By adopting a growth mindset and investing in your development as a negotiator, you can elevate your leadership effectiveness and achieve your business objectives.

Questions and Action:

1. Reflect on past negotiations in your professional life. What strategies were effective in achieving your desired outcomes, and what lessons did you learn from less successful negotiations?

2. Consider how negotiation skills can be applied to everyday business decisions, such as vendor contracts, employee negotiations, and strategic partnerships. What opportunities exist to leverage negotiation as a strategic tool in your role?

3. Identify specific areas for improvement in your negotiation skills and develop an action plan to enhance your effectiveness as a negotiator. Set measurable goals, seek feedback from peers and mentors, and commit to continuous growth and development.

Case Study 3: MESO, Negotiation, and Dealing with Difficult People

Case Study: Imagine you're a project manager overseeing a cross-functional team tasked with developing a new product for your company. As the project progresses, tensions arise between two key team members: Sarah, the lead engineer, and David, the marketing manager. Sarah is focused on technical specifications and prioritizing functionality, while David is concerned with marketability and customer appeal. Their conflicting priorities lead to frequent disagreements and impede progress on the project.

Explanation: In situations like this, employing the Multiple Equivalent Simultaneous Offers (MESO) negotiation strategy can help break through deadlocks and foster collaboration. By presenting multiple options that address the interests of both parties, you can encourage constructive dialogue and find a mutually acceptable solution. MESO provides a framework for overcoming interpersonal conflicts and moving negotiations forward effectively.

Key Takeaways: Dealing with difficult people in negotiations requires patience, empathy, and strategic thinking. By embracing negotiation techniques like MESO, you can navigate challenging dynamics, build consensus, and achieve positive outcomes. Remember to focus on interests rather than positions and explore creative solutions that meet the needs of all parties involved.

Application: When faced with difficult people or challenging negotiations, consider employing the MESO strategy to explore multiple options and facilitate productive discussions. Practice active listening, ask open-ended questions, and seek to understand the underlying interests driving the conflict. By fostering a collaborative environment and demonstrating flexibility, you can foster trust and find common ground with even the most challenging counterparts.

Questions and Action:

1. Reflect on past experiences of dealing with difficult people in negotiations or team settings. What strategies were effective in

resolving conflicts, and what lessons did you learn from these experiences?

2. Explore how the MESO negotiation strategy could be applied to your current or future negotiation challenges. What options could you present to address the interests of all parties involved?

3. Identify opportunities to practice active listening and empathy in your interactions with difficult individuals. How can you create an environment that encourages open dialogue and constructive problem-solving?

Case Study 4: Family Conflict Resolution Lessons from the Home

Case Study: Imagine you're a manager overseeing a team of employees who have been experiencing interpersonal conflicts and tensions in the workplace. As you investigate the root causes of these conflicts, you discover that many of the team members are struggling with communication issues, personality clashes, and unresolved grievances. Some team members avoid confrontation, while others escalate conflicts, creating a toxic work environment.

Explanation: Drawing parallels between family dynamics and workplace conflicts can provide valuable insights into effective conflict resolution strategies. Just as families navigate disagreements and maintain harmony, teams can learn from techniques like active listening, empathy, and compromise to address conflict constructively. By fostering a culture of respect, trust, and open communication, leaders can mitigate conflict and promote collaboration within their teams.

Key Takeaways: Conflict resolution skills honed in family settings can be applied to the workplace to promote a positive organizational culture. By adopting a compassionate and empathetic approach, leaders can create an environment where team members feel heard, valued, and supported. Encouraging open dialogue, acknowledging diverse perspectives, and seeking win-win solutions can transform conflicts into opportunities for growth and collaboration.

Application: Reflect on your experiences managing conflicts within your team and identify strategies inspired by family conflict resolution techniques. Practice active listening, empathy, and conflict mediation skills to address interpersonal tensions and promote a harmonious work environment. By modeling positive conflict resolution behaviors and fostering a culture of collaboration, you can create a workplace where differences are celebrated and conflicts are resolved constructively.

Questions and Action:

1. Reflect on your family's approach to resolving conflicts. What lessons can you apply to your leadership role in managing workplace conflicts?

2. Explore opportunities to incorporate family-inspired conflict resolution techniques into your team's dynamics. How can you encourage open communication and mutual respect among team members?

3. Identify one conflict resolution strategy inspired by family dynamics that you can implement in your team. How will you promote a culture of empathy, understanding, and collaboration?

Case Study 5: Navigating Generational Differences in the Workplace

Case Study: Imagine you're a team leader in a dynamic workplace environment, where employees from different generations collaborate on projects and initiatives. One of your team members, Sarah, frequently clashes with older colleagues due to differences in work styles, communication preferences, and technology use. These conflicts create tension within the team, hinder collaboration, and impact overall productivity.

Explanation: Addressing intergenerational conflicts in the workplace requires a nuanced understanding of each generation's perspectives, values, and communication styles. Leaders must navigate generational differences with empathy, respect, and an open-minded approach to foster collaboration and harmony within diverse teams. By recognizing the unique strengths and contributions of each generation, leaders can bridge divides, promote mutual understanding, and build cohesive teams.

Key Takeaways: Successfully navigating generational differences requires empathy, adaptability, and effective communication. Leaders should foster a culture of inclusivity, respect, and appreciation for diverse perspectives to harness the collective talents of multigenerational teams. By leveraging the unique strengths and experiences of each generation, leaders can foster collaboration, innovation, and organizational success.

Application: Reflect on your experiences leading multigenerational teams and identify opportunities to promote understanding and collaboration across generations. Encourage open dialogue, mutual respect, and knowledge sharing to bridge generational divides and foster a culture of inclusivity and belonging. By embracing diversity and leveraging the strengths of each generation, you can create a thriving workplace environment where all employees feel valued and empowered.

Questions and Action:

1. Reflect on your interactions with colleagues from different generations. What insights

have you gained about their perspectives, communication styles, and work preferences?

2. Explore opportunities to promote intergenerational collaboration and knowledge sharing within your team or organization. How can you leverage the unique strengths of each generation to enhance team performance and innovation?

3. Identify one initiative or project where intergenerational collaboration could lead to better outcomes. Develop a plan to facilitate dialogue, foster understanding, and promote collaboration among team members from different generations.

Case Study 6: Dispute Resolution Through Joint Fact-Finding

Case Study: Imagine you're a project manager overseeing a complex construction project with multiple stakeholders and competing interests. As the project progresses, disagreements arise over design specifications, resource allocations, and project timelines, leading to delays and cost overruns. Despite efforts to resolve conflicts through traditional negotiation channels, disputes persist, jeopardizing the project's success and stakeholder relationships.

Explanation: In complex disputes involving multiple parties and divergent interests, traditional negotiation approaches may prove insufficient to reach a resolution. Joint fact-finding offers a collaborative framework for exploring shared interests, identifying underlying concerns, and developing mutually acceptable solutions. By engaging neutral third parties and leveraging objective data and analysis, stakeholders can gain clarity, build trust, and pave the way for effective dispute resolution.

Key Takeaways: Resolving complex disputes requires a multifaceted approach that goes beyond traditional negotiation tactics. Joint fact-finding provides a structured process for uncovering common ground, addressing information gaps, and fostering consensus among stakeholders. By embracing transparency, collaboration, and open-mindedness, parties can overcome barriers to agreement and achieve sustainable outcomes.

Application: Reflect on your experiences managing complex disputes or conflicts involving multiple stakeholders and identify opportunities to apply joint fact-finding techniques. Engage neutral third parties, facilitate information sharing, and encourage collaborative problem-solving to address underlying issues and build consensus. By adopting a fact-based and collaborative approach, you can navigate challenging disputes and foster productive relationships among stakeholders.

Questions and Action:

1. Reflect on a challenging dispute or conflict you've encountered in your professional experience. How could joint fact-finding have helped uncover shared interests and facilitate resolution?

2. Explore opportunities to engage neutral third parties and conduct collaborative fact-finding processes in your current or future dispute resolution efforts. What stakeholders could benefit from a fact-based approach to resolving conflicts?

3. Identify one dispute or conflict within your organization that could benefit from joint fact-finding. Develop a plan to initiate a collaborative process and engage relevant parties in exploring shared interests and finding common ground.

Case Study 7: Resolving Conflicts in a Family-Owned Business

Case Study: Picture yourself as a member of a family-owned business that has been operating for generations. The company's success is built on strong familial bonds, shared values, and a commitment to excellence. However, recent disagreements among family members regarding business decisions, succession planning, and leadership roles have created tension and conflict within the organization. These disputes threaten to undermine the company's cohesion, profitability, and long-term sustainability.

Explanation: Resolving conflicts in a family-owned business requires delicacy, empathy, and a strategic approach to navigating complex interpersonal dynamics. Leaders must balance familial relationships with business imperatives, fostering open communication, mutual respect, and shared decision-making. By establishing clear processes for conflict resolution, setting aside personal differences, and focusing on the common goals and values that unite the family, leaders can mitigate conflicts and ensure the continued success and prosperity of the business.

Key Takeaways: Successful conflict resolution in a family-owned business hinges on effective communication, mutual respect, and a commitment to shared goals. Leaders must prioritize transparency, fairness, and inclusivity, fostering an environment where all family members feel heard, valued, and empowered. By addressing conflicts proactively, cultivating trust, and upholding the family's legacy of excellence, leaders can navigate challenges and strengthen the resilience of the business.

Application: Reflect on the unique dynamics of your family-owned business and identify areas where conflicts may arise. Develop strategies to promote open dialogue, foster collaboration, and address conflicts constructively, drawing on shared values and a collective vision for the future. By fostering a culture of trust, respect, and resilience, you can uphold the legacy of your family business and ensure its continued success across generations.

Questions and Action:

1. Reflect on past conflicts within your family-owned business. What were the underlying causes, and how were they resolved?

2. Explore opportunities to enhance communication and collaboration among family members, particularly in areas where conflicts may arise. How can you promote transparency, fairness, and inclusivity in decision-making processes?

3. Develop a conflict resolution plan tailored to the unique needs and dynamics of your family business. How can you establish clear processes, roles, and responsibilities for addressing conflicts and fostering unity within the organization?

Case Study 8: Negotiating Vendor Contracts

Case Study: Imagine you're a procurement manager for a mid-sized company tasked with negotiating vendor contracts for essential supplies. Your company relies on these vendors to maintain operations and meet customer demand, making contract negotiations a critical aspect of your role. However, recent changes in market conditions, supply chain disruptions, and rising costs have complicated negotiations with existing vendors and made it challenging to secure favorable terms for future contracts.

Explanation: Negotiating vendor contracts requires a strategic approach, effective communication, and a keen understanding of market dynamics and vendor capabilities. As a procurement manager, your goal is to secure mutually beneficial agreements that meet the company's needs while maintaining positive relationships with vendors. By conducting thorough market research, analyzing vendor proposals, and leveraging negotiation techniques such as cost-benefit analysis and value-based bargaining, you can optimize contract terms and achieve optimal outcomes for your organization.

Key Takeaways: Successful negotiation of vendor contracts hinges on thorough preparation, clear communication, and a focus on value creation. Procurement managers must assess the company's requirements, evaluate vendor offerings, and negotiate terms that align with strategic objectives and budget constraints. By building trust, fostering collaboration, and seeking win-win solutions, procurement managers can strengthen vendor relationships and drive long-term business success.

Application: Reflect on your current approach to negotiating vendor contracts and identify areas for improvement. Develop a negotiation strategy that incorporates market insights, stakeholder input, and best practices in contract management. By adopting a proactive and collaborative approach to vendor negotiations, you can optimize contract terms, mitigate risks, and enhance the value proposition for your organization.

Questions and Action:

1. What are the key factors influencing vendor negotiations in your industry, and how are they impacting your procurement strategy?

2. How can you leverage data analytics and market intelligence to inform your negotiation tactics and achieve better outcomes in vendor contracts?

3. What steps can you take to strengthen relationships with key vendors and enhance collaboration in contract negotiations?

In this section, we delved into real-world case studies that exemplify the principles and techniques of effective conflict resolution. From navigating cultural differences in negotiations to resolving disputes through joint fact-finding, each case study provided valuable insights into the dynamics of conflict and demonstrated how strategic approaches can lead to positive outcomes.

Through these case studies, we witnessed the importance of preparation, communication, and collaboration in resolving conflicts and reaching mutually beneficial agreements.

Whether dealing with interpersonal disputes in the workplace or complex negotiations in business settings, the principles of conflict resolution remain consistent: understanding different perspectives, exploring creative solutions, and fostering constructive dialogue.

As we conclude this section, it's essential to reflect on the key lessons learned from these case studies. By applying the principles of effective conflict resolution, individuals and organizations can build stronger relationships, enhance productivity, and create a culture of collaboration and innovation.

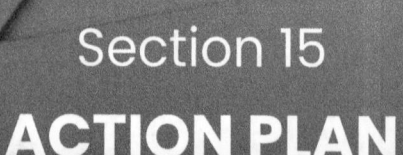

Section 15

ACTION PLAN

Alright, yall, we've had quite the journey, haven't we? We've learned about the ins and outs of conflict, discovered our own unique conflict navigation styles, and explored a range of strategies and techniques for managing disputes. We've even dipped our toes into the waters of real-life case studies. But now, it's time for the grand finale – your very own action plan.

This section is all about taking the theory and turning it into practice. Don't worry; I'm not going to leave you hanging. Together, we'll create a step-by-step blueprint to guide you through your future conflicts, ensuring you're well-equipped to navigate any tricky situation life throws you.

Step 1: Self-reflection Before you jump into any conflict, take a moment to reflect.

- What's your conflict navigation style?

- What are your strengths and weaknesses when it comes to managing disputes? By understanding yourself better, you'll be more able to handle conflicts effectively.

Step 2: Understand the Conflict. Next, get a clear understanding of what the conflict is about.

- What's the root cause? Who are the involved parties?

- What are their interests, needs, and concerns? Remember, conflicts aren't always as simple as they seem on the surface. Dig a little deeper.

Step 3: Choose your Strategy. Decide on the best strategy based on your understanding of the conflict and your own conflict navigation style. Should you go for Team Builder, or is this a situation where Harmonizer might work better?

Remember, different conflicts call for different strategies.

- What are the potential outcomes of this conflict?

- Which strategy would be the most effective based on your understanding of the conflict and your conflict style? Why?

Step 4: Prepare for Negotiation Before entering the negotiation phase, ensure you are well-prepared. Identify your goals, establish your boundaries, and decide on your negotiation tactics. Preparation is key to successful conflict resolution.

- What are your primary goals for this negotiation? What are your secondary goals?

- What boundaries have you set for this negotiation?

- What negotiation tactics would be the most beneficial for this specific conflict?

Step 5: Engage in the Conflict Now, it's time to jump into the fray. Keeping your emotions in check, communicating clearly and effectively, and keeping the end goal in sight. Remember, conflict isn't about winning or losing but finding a solution that works for everyone.

- How did you handle your emotions during the conflict?

- Did your communication remain clear and effective throughout the conflict? If not, where could you improve?

- Did you keep your end goal in mind during the conflict?

Step 6: Reflect and Learn. Once the conflict is resolved, don't just move on. Take some time to reflect. What did you learn? How could you have handled things better? What will you do differently next time? By learning from each conflict, you'll navigate conflict more effectively.

- What lessons have you learned from this conflict? How could you have handled things better?

- What will you do differently in your next conflict based on this experience?

- Alright, time to roll up those sleeves and get to work! With this action plan, you're ready to take on any conflict that comes your way.

Remember, the path to becoming an expert conflict navigator isn't a straight line. It's a journey of learning, growth, and constant improvement. So, keep this guide handy, revisit it often, and keep practicing your skills. Good luck, and here's to becoming a pro at navigating conflicts!

Section 16

FOLLOW-UP ACTIONS

Resolving a conflict doesn't mean crossing the finish line. It's like passing the baton in a relay race. That's where follow-up actions come in, keeping the resolution momentum going and making sure everyone sticks to their part of the deal.

Here's how to nail your follow-up actions:

- **Clear Action Steps:** Everyone involved should know exactly what they need to do next. Like a good to-do list, these steps should be Specific, Measurable, Achievable, Relevant, and Time-bound (SMART).

- **Accountability:** Just like a fitness buddy who keeps you on your toes, you need a system that holds everyone accountable for their actions. Regular check-ins or progress reports can do the trick.

- **Review and Adjust:** It's all about staying flexible. After putting the solutions to work, take a step back, review how things are going, and tweak the plan as needed.

Let's take a moment to reflect: How often do you think about what happens after a conflict is resolved? How can you make sure everyone sticks to their part of the agreement?

Mastering feedback and follow-up actions is like learning the choreography to a dance. Once you've got the moves down, you'll not only resolve conflicts but also learn, grow, and improve from each experience.

Section 17

MASTERING THE ART OF RECEIVING AND USING FEEDBACK

Feedback – it's like a compass in the wilderness of conflict resolution, guiding us towards improvement. But let's be real: not all feedback makes us want to break into a happy dance. Sometimes, it's as welcome as a mosquito at a barbecue. Yet, it's crucial for growth. In this section, we'll explore how to not only accept feedback but to use it as a powerful tool for enhancing your conflict resolution skills.

1. **Understanding Feedback Triggers**: Feedback can trigger emotional responses, especially when it hits a nerve. Common triggers include truth triggers (feedback feels off-base), relationship triggers (who's giving the feedback matters), and identity triggers (feedback hits at the core of who we are). Recognizing these triggers helps us respond more rationally and less defensively (Stone & Heen, 2014).

2. **Active Listening in Feedback**: Treat feedback like a gold mine. Listen actively. Don't just wait to respond or defend yourself. Ask questions for clarity. Remember, behind every piece of feedback is a perception or a personal experience worth understanding.

3. **Reflecting on Feedback**: Don't just take feedback at face value. Reflect on it. Does it resonate with experiences or patterns you've noticed? Could there be a kernel of truth in it, even if it's delivered poorly?

4. **Actionable Steps Post-Feedback**: Turn feedback into action. Identify specific areas you can work on. Set small, achievable goals. Maybe it's practicing active listening or keeping your cool in heated moments.

5. **Creating a Feedback-Friendly Environment**: Encourage a culture where feedback is part of the norm – not just top-down but peer-to-peer, too. It's like creating a garden where feedback can bloom into growth and learning.

6. **Dealing with Contradictory Feedback**: When feedback is as mixed as a bag of nuts, look for patterns. Contradictory feedback can be confusing, but it often highlights areas that need more attention or different approaches.

Remember, feedback isn't just about pointing out what's wrong. It's an opportunity for growth, for fine-tuning your skills, and for becoming a conflict resolution ninja. So, next time you receive feedback, take a deep breath, embrace it, and use it to steer your conflict resolution ship to new horizons.

Section 18

REFLECTION QUESTIONS

Now that we've taken a deep dive into the ocean of conflict management, it's time to anchor in some reflection. This section is your opportunity to draw personal connections between the concepts, strategies, and case studies we've explored and your own experiences with conflict.

Reflection is the lighthouse in your journey, illuminating your understanding and guiding your future actions. It's the process where learning gets personal and knowledge transforms into wisdom. So, take a moment, take a breath, and dive into these questions with an open mind and an honest heart.

1. Conflict Understanding

- What was the nature of the last conflict you experienced? What were the core issues at play in this conflict?

- How did you react to the conflict, and why do you think you reacted in that way?

2. Conflict Navigation Styles

- Which of the conflict navigation styles do you tend to use most often?

- Can you identify a time when you used each of the different styles? What was the outcome?

- What situations or types of conflicts might call for a different navigation style than the one you typically use?

3. Conflict Strategy and Negotiation

- How do you typically approach negotiation in a conflict situation?

- Can you identify a time when a negotiation strategy worked well for you? What about a time when it didn't work?

- How might you alter your negotiation strategy for different types of conflicts or different individuals?

4. Case Studies

- Which case study resonated most with you, and why?

- How might you apply the lessons from these case studies to your own conflict situations?

- Are there any aspects of these case studies that you disagree with or find challenging to apply in your context?

5. Action Plan

- What does your ideal conflict resolution process look like, based on what you've learned?

- What steps will you take the next time you're faced with a conflict situation?

- How will you continue to develop and refine your conflict resolution skills moving forward?

Remember, the goal of these questions is to encourage introspection and self- awareness. Honest answers to these questions can be a powerful tool for personal and professional growth.

CONCLUSION

CHARTING YOUR COURSE

And there you have it - your compass to navigate the stormy seas of conflict. By now, you should better understand conflict, your approach to it, some strategies for effective negotiation, and even a few case studies to inspire your journey.

But remember, mastering conflict resolution isn't a one-and-done deal. It's a continuous journey of learning, growing, and adapting. Every conflict is a new opportunity to apply these strategies, refine your skills, and grow as a person. As you continue on your path, let these lessons be your North Star, guiding you towards more meaningful, productive interactions, even in the face of conflict.

So, sailor, it's time to set sail. May your journey be filled with self-discovery, growth, and smoother sailing.

Fair winds and following seas.

REFERENCES

1. Stone, D., & Heen, S. (2014). Thanks for the feedback: The science and art of receiving feedback well. Viking.